ACCOUNTING JOB QUESTIONS AND ANSWERS

Trainee Accountants Handbook

Sterling Libs FCCA

Accounting Job Questions and Answers
Copyright © 2018 by Sterling Libs. All rights reserved.

www.sterlinglibs.com

London, United Kingdom

No part of this publication may be reproduced, stored in a retrieval system, or transmitted in any form or by any means – electronic, mechanical, photocopy, recording, or any other – except for brief quotations in printed reviews, without the prior permission of the Author/Publisher

All rights reserved.

ISBN: 978-1-911037-12-5

NOTE TO READER

At its most basic level, practical accounting involves the analysis and recording/processing of business financial transactions then producing reports summarising the financial performance of a business. It's a crucial operational part of almost every business, and most companies have at least one accountant or bookkeeper who manages the organisation's financial records.

However, the accounting profession encompasses much more than just data entry and financial reporting.

As an accountant, you may provide a broad range of income tax and consulting services, prepare and analyse budgets and conduct internal and external audits.
Many accountants go on to be leaders in the business world because of their backgrounds in finance.

Through this book, I hope to help you build a foundation in accounting that will eventually help you succeed as a leader in the business world as you grow and mature in the profession.

Contents

ACCOUNTING JOB QUESTIONS AND ANSWERS i
INTRODUCTION i
THE ACCOUNTING JOB 3
    Common accounting jobs 5
        The 10 most common accounting jobs/roles 7
ACCOUNTING JOB QUESTIONS & ANSWERS 15
    What is the main difference between a tax year & a financial year 15
    What is a Tax return? 15
    What is PAYE and when does a business have to register for PAYE? 16
    What is VAT and when does a business have to register for VAT? 16
    What would you say every business is fundamentally involved in doing? 17
    Describe the Accounts Payable (AP) process? 18
    What is a Credit note? 24
    Describe the Accounts Receivable (AR) process? 25
    How do you produce financial reports from financial documents? 29
    Whose responsibility is it to submit annual accounts to government authorities? 38
    How do you present the two primary financial statements? 38
    The format of a simple management account profit & Loss statement 42
HOW DO YOU ANSWER TRICKY TECHNICAL JOB INTERVIEW QUESTIONS? 47
    7 Accountant Interview Questions and Answers 50
HOW TO GET AND KEEP AN ACCOUNTING JOB 53
    The Top five things you should put on your CV 55
    The Top five things to do during an interview 56
WHY SOME PEOPLE STRUGGLE TO GET ACCOUNTING JOBS & WHAT TO DO ABOUT IT 57
    7 things you can do to help you get an accounting job quickly 58
AFTERWORD 61
ABOUT THE AUTHOR 62

INTRODUCTION

As an accountant, you can work in the private or public sector, for small or large businesses or even for the government. You may also choose to work on an individual level on a self-employed basis, doing anything from auditing and filing tax returns to budgeting and financial planning.

Some accountants even specialise in more unique areas of accounting like environmental accounting; which involves analysing the impacts business operations have on the environment; such as the financial damage from ecological disasters, or forensic accounting; which involves fraud prevention and detection.

Your chances of finding work as an accountant are significantly high as there will always be a need for accountants.

You see, regardless of how well the economy is doing, organisations need financial experts to maintain their financial records. Without accounting, it would be a tough call for companies to comply with all the tax laws out there, to judge their success (or failure) and to plan for the future.

What's important to know as well is that different sectors and employers all have their advantages and disadvantages – you have to decide what suits your personality and career aspirations best.

The information in this book will be of enormous help to you as you seek to understand your place in the world as an accountant.

"Only a life lived for others is a life worthwhile"

Albert Einstein

"There is safety in accountability. Have an accountability partner."
Sterling Libs

THE ACCOUNTING JOB

The theoretical studies of accounting are essential to prepare you for work in industry and practice in the real world. Where there is business, there will be a need for the services of an accountant one way or the other.

Accounting is a principle-based profession in that some standards and principles govern how accountants should operate and do their work.

What I have done in this book is ask a series of questions and provide answers to the same in such a way that I highlight the main aspects of the principles you should know when you are engaged in working as an accountant in industry & practice during your career in the accounting profession.

I have covered both the theoretical and practical aspects of accounting in such a way that throughout the time you read the book, you keep your interest and attention engaged.

The questions and corresponding answers in this book will help you to have a coherent view and understanding of accounting in practice and will enormously help with your confidence during job interviews.
Let's have a look at what a typical job description of an accountant looks like.

Some of the most common regular accounting tasks you will be involved in doing in your career as an accountant are:

At a junior level;

- ✓ Processing customer invoices and receipts
- ✓ Collecting outstanding amounts from debtors
- ✓ Processing supplier invoices & supplier payments
- ✓ Supplier statement reconciliations
- ✓ Payroll processing and posting payroll journals
- ✓ Sorting out; the post and providing clerical support to management
- ✓ Bank reconciliation
- ✓ VAT Return preparation and submission to HMRC
- ✓ Managing petty cash
- ✓ Answering phones and ordering stationery
- ✓ Assisting with credit control
- ✓ Doing month end accounting procedures
- ✓ Yearend accounts preparation
- ✓ Preparing Tax returns & submitting them to HMRC

And at a senior level:

- ✓ Examining statements to ensure accuracy
- ✓ Ensuring that statements and records comply with laws and regulations
- ✓ Computing taxes owed, prepare tax returns, ensure prompt payment
- ✓ Inspecting account books and accounting systems to keep up to date
- ✓ Organising and maintaining financial records
- ✓ Improving businesses efficiency where money is concerned
- ✓ Making best-practice recommendations to management
- ✓ Suggesting ways to reduce costs, enhance revenues and improve profits
- ✓ Providing auditing services for businesses and individuals

If you have a job or are looking for a job, the chances are that you will be working for or in one of the following legal entities that business are required to operate in the UK:

- ✓ Sole Trader
- ✓ Partnership
- ✓ Company limited by shares (LTD)
- ✓ Designated Activity Company (DAC)

- ✓ Company limited by guarantee (CLG) – Charity
- ✓ Limited Liability Partnership (LLP)
- ✓ Community Interest Company (CIC)
- ✓ Public Listed company (PLC)

It is important that you understand the reporting and regulatory requirements for the business entity you work in to avoid making mistakes and thus jeopardise your career.

Now, without further ado, let's look at some questions and answers to help broaden your understanding of accounting in practice and give you some confidence when attending accounting job interviews.
Let's begin.

Let's look at specific accounting jobs, and how to get them, then we will look at some of the common terms, questions and answers that you will need to get familiar with if you are not already.

Common accounting jobs

There are three main branches of accounting – Financial accounting, Management accounting and Cost accounting. Most accounting jobs out there will be within these three branches.

Let's briefly look at what each branch of accounting has to offer.

Financial accounting

The primary objective of financial accounting is the preparation of financial statements – including the balance sheet, income statement and cash flow statement – that encapsulates the company's operating performance over a particular period, and financial position at a specific point in time. These statements – which are generally prepared quarterly and annually, and in accordance with Generally Accepted Accounting Principles (GAAP) – are aimed at external parties including investors, creditors, regulators and tax authorities.

Management Accounting
Managerial accounting is the process of identifying, measuring, analysing, interpreting and communicating information for the pursuit of an organisation's goals.

It is focused on the interpretation of accounting information to help the management in future planning, decision making, control, etc. Management accountancy, for that reason, serves the information requirements of the insiders, e.g., owners, managers and employees.

The key difference between managerial and financial accounting is managerial accounting information is aimed at helping managers within the organisation make decisions, while financial accounting is aimed at providing information to parties outside the organisation.

Cost accounting

Cost accounting is a type of accounting process that aims to capture a company's costs of production by assessing the input costs of each step of production as well as fixed costs such as depreciation of capital equipment. Cost accounting will first measure and record these costs individually, then compare input results to output or actual results to aid company management in measuring financial performance.

While cost accounting is often used within a company to aid in decision making, financial accounting is what the outside investor community typically sees. Financial accounting is a different representation of costs and financial performance that includes a company's assets and liabilities. Cost accounting can be most beneficial as a tool for management in budgeting and in setting up cost control programs, which can improve net margins for the company in the future.

One key difference between cost accounting and financial accounting is that while in financial accounting the cost is classified depending on the type of transaction, cost accounting classifies costs according to the information needs of the management. Cost accounting, because it is used as an internal tool by management, does not have to meet any specific standard set by the Generally Accepted Accounting Principles (GAAP) and as a result varies in use from company to company or from department to department.

With that brief introduction to the main three branches of accounting (Financial, Management & Cost accounting), we can now look at some of the most common accounting jobs/roles available in the market.
We will look at the job descriptions, the person specifications and the key skills required to do the jobs.

As a professional accountant, the chances of you finding work are significantly high as successful companies will always need accounting staff to work in their finance departments.

Different sectors and employers all have their own advantages and disadvantages – you have to decide what suits your personality and career aspirations best.

"The secret of getting ahead is getting started". **Mark Twain**

The 10 most common accounting jobs/roles

I will give you one tip that will certainly help you get a job - ASK for it. If you see an accounting job you feel you can do, just ask for it. There are many ways you can ask for a job – by applying for it, through a referral, etc., But ASK you must.

"Ask, and it will be given to you; seek and you will find; knock, and it will be opened to you. For everyone who asks receives, and he who seeks finds, and to him who knocks it will be opened". **Jesus Christ**

In no particular order of importance, here are the ten most common accounting jobs/roles that you could potentially choose as a career path.

1. **Finance Manager**

Job profile: As a finance manager, you'll work with all departments of the business to help them plan and manage their budgets. You'll also work closely with the CEO to help him/her manage the overall business so it makes the most money it can.

Where you work will have an impact on the work you do. In a bigger company the role is often more strategic and involves much analysis, and you might be the finance director for a division rather than for the whole company. If you work for a smaller company, you'll probably have to be a bit more hands-on with general accounts matters too.

It's a broad and exciting role covering activities like:

- Monitoring cash flow
- Supervising your own accounts team
- Monitoring business performance

- Developing financial models
- Preparing accounts
- Overseeing the budgets and that everyone is sticking to them
- Working with departments and teams
- Planning for the future
- Competitor analysis
- Strategic planning

Average salary: £53,660 (GMB/ONS)

2. Management Accountant

Job profile: Management accountants look to the future rather than the past when assessing the financial status of an organisation. Their role is to provide the financial information necessary to enable an organisation's management team to make sound strategic decisions.

Some organisations will have their own management accountants. You could also work for a private accountancy firm which offers accountancy services to fee-paying clients.

The kind of activities you'll oversee include:

- Making sure spending is in line with budgets
- Recommending ways of cutting costs
- Analysing your company's financial performance and making longer-term forecasts
- Providing information for audits
- Working with all departments and the management team to help make financial decisions

A big focus of your job will be to make sure the business is compliant with financial governance requirements.

You'll most likely manage a team who will help you with all your duties although the role does vary quite widely depending on the size of the business and what sector it is in.

Average salary: Typical starting salary is £21,000, £30,000-£45,000 with experience rising to £60,000+ for the senior position (CIMA)

3. Auditor

Job profile: As an auditor, your job is to ensure that an organisation is using its resources in the most efficient ways – whether for the sake of the taxpayer in the public sector, or shareholders in private businesses.

You are responsible for auditing the accounts of an organisation, analysing expenditure and its effectiveness, assessing risks to financial control and accountability.

You'll not only have to write reports on your findings, but you may also find yourself in a boardroom giving PowerPoint presentations to managers and directors. You'll be expected to keep on top of the many changes in the law and keep a rational view of the best way ahead when all around you, people are flapping in a panic.

You will in many instances need strong communication skills, lots of tact, and confidence in your own ability.

Average salary: On a graduate trainee scheme straight out of college, your starting salary will be £18,000-£22,000 a year. Once you're fully- fledged, an auditor can expect to earn £35,000-£45,000 in a public sector position, rising to well over £60,000 as a senior audit manager. £49,072 - £63,235 is the average according to National Audit Office.

4. Tax Adviser

Job profile: As a tax adviser, you will provide a professional advisory and consultancy service to clients, interpret complicated tax legislation (and its implications to the client) and plan the best strategy to plan clients' financial affairs and minimise future tax liabilities.

You could work for an accountancy firm, a specialist tax consultancy or a company with its own tax team. Banks, legal firms and HM Revenue and Customs also need good tax specialists.

You could also choose to become a freelance tax consultant and start your own business. Why not?
The typical duties to perform in this role will include but not limited to:

- Researching and understanding tax law

- Liaising with HM Revenue and Customs on your clients' behalf
- Checking and completing tax forms
- Meeting clients to gather information and explain options available to them
- Auditing clients' tax records

Individuals, small businesses and large companies all need good, clear and simple tax advice. So your job is really a very important one and one you should cherish.

Salary: Starting salary of Tax Adviser is at £20,000-£37,000 rising to £30,000-£55,000 upon obtaining the ATT qualification (ATT) or even £65,000 plus with the CTA qualification and substantial experience.

5. Credit Controller

Job profile: This is primarily an office-based role where you'll be expected to work 9:00 am -5:00 pm, Monday to Friday with some overtime at busy periods such as the end of the year. The beauty of this role is that credit control principles are the same whatever industry you work in and you can move into different sectors. With enough experience, you could even become the go-to person – consultant.

It will be your responsibility to review debt recovery procedures and stop the supply of goods and services - or even start the serious process of legal action - if a client has paid late or missed multiple payments. It's not the nicest part of the job, but someone's got to do it. You may be required to attend meetings with clients or occasionally court hearings if you're taking legal action against a client.

Generally, your role will include performing the following tasks:

- Ensuring customers pay on time
- Setting up the terms and conditions of credit to customers
- Deciding whether or not to offer the credit and how much to offer to a client
- Checking customer's credit ratings with banks
- Negotiating re-payment plans
- Dealing with internal queries about payments

Salary: The starting salary for a credit controller can range between £17,000 and £28,000 per year but this can rise to over £45,000 plus if you move up the ladder to become a credit control manager.

6. Accounts Assistant

Job profile: As an Accounts Assistant, you will provide administrative support to accountants, handling mail and basic bookkeeping and undertaking clerical tasks such as making phone calls, typing, and filing.

Depending on the size of the organisation you work for, the tasks you will be performing include but not limited to:

- Assisting with all aspects of sales & purchase ledger
- Assisting with the preparation of statutory accounts.
- Assisting with credit control and debtor management.
- Calculating and checking to make sure payments, amounts and records are correct.
- Working with spreadsheets and journals.
- Sorting out the incoming and outgoing daily post and answering any queries.
- Managing petty cash transactions.
- Reconciling finance accounts and direct debits.
- Assisting with payroll and posting payroll journals

Salary: Accounts assistants earn an average of £18,500 – £22,000 a year (for full-time hours), but the starting salary can be as little as £13,000 for inexperienced employees.

7. Bookkeeper

Job profile: Most of the time you'll work 9 am to 5 pm, Monday to Friday. There may be the odd times when it's really quite busy (like during yearend), and you need to work a few extra hours.

Your main role is to maintain financial records for the company and to do your job effectively you ought to have a detail-oriented approach to work that will allow you to keep up with company expenditures, income, and payroll as well as tax requirements.

There are positions across a wide range of organisations, so it's up to you to choose an industry you are interested in - health, public sector, private sector, charities etc.

There are opportunities for part-time and job sharing. Temporary work is often available too. You could also work freelance to work the hours that suit you.

The larger the company you work for, the more opportunities for progression there will be.

With experience and sufficient professional qualifications, you could choose to be self-employed or set up your own company supporting several smaller businesses.

Salary: For a new starter you can expect to earn between £12,000 and £14,000 a year. As you get more experience you'll be able to earn up to £20,000. On average, for an experienced and qualified bookkeeper salary can be £23,000-£27,500 (Association for Accounting Technicians)

8. Sales Ledger Clerk

Job profile: Sales ledger clerks form the administrative side of an accounting team. You'll spend most of your time at your desk raising invoices and talking to clients.
This job is ideal for you if you want a career that offers room to move as there's plenty of scope for promotion once you've got some experience. Sales ledger clerks often graduate to work as a supervisor or manager and from there to credit controller and even financial controller.

Your main duties will include:

- Setting up new clients
- Producing invoices
- Sorting out any rebates, posts and filing
- Running off turnover statements
- Banking and reconciliation
- Checking sales VAT has been included on invoices
- Chasing up outstanding debts

Salary: Starting salary can be around £18,000 to £20,000. This will increase to £30,000 plus once you take on a more supervisory role.

9. Purchase ledger clerk

Job profile: Typical work hours are 9:00 am – 5:00 pm Monday to Friday. Your responsibilities will depend on the size of the company you work for, and you may have sole control over payments or work as part of a much bigger purchase ledger team. Purchase ledger clerks are expected to be able to:

- Code and check supplier invoices
- Work out VAT payments
- Check and reconcile supplier statements
- Payout money via BACS or by cheque
- Deal with purchase enquiries
- File invoices and statements
- Process staff expenses
- Manage petty cash

Salary: As a starter, you should expect your salary to range from £16,000-£23,000 per year, depending on your experience and qualifications.

10. Payroll Administrator

Job profile: You'll be involved with creating new payroll policies and procedures, reporting back to the management team and ensuring all the computer systems are up to date in terms of government legislation like RTI, pensions etc.

As part of the payroll administration team the duties that you will perform include but are not limited to the following:

- Checking people's hours
- Making the weekly or monthly salary/wage payments on time
- Issuing pay slips to employees
- Working out tax and national insurance deductions
- Submitting the payroll report to HMRC
- Providing the accountants with the payroll journal figures to be posted into the accounts
- Setting up new members of staff on the payroll
- Calculating overtime
- Issuing tax forms (P45s, P60, etc.)
- Managing special situations like maternity or sickness, holiday

You could work as part of the payroll team in an organisation or for a payroll bureau – a company that specialises in running the payroll for other companies.

Average salary: If you're just starting as a payroll administrator you should be on £13,000 to £18,000 a year. This jumps up to £20,000 and £25,000 as you get more qualified and more experienced.

Do you lack practical work experience?

In many cases, a progressive career in accountancy requires that you have sufficient work experience. If you are based in the UK and need to gain practical work experience in accountancy, TD&A Certified Accountants may be able to help you. Click here or visit their website at http://www.tdanda.co.uk/careers

> "Money is hidden in relationships and moves freely in relationships. Enhance and broaden your relationships everyday otherwise pretty soon you will be broke"
>
> **Sterling Libs**

"Don't be afraid to wipe the slate clean and start all over again. Sometimes, that is the only best option."

Sterling Libs

ACCOUNTING JOB QUESTIONS & ANSWERS

What is the main difference between a tax year & a financial year

- A tax year in the UK is from the 6th of April current year to the following 5th April next year.
- A financial (fiscal) year, on the other hand, commences on the date a business starts trading and runs for 12 months. A company's fiscal year can straddle two tax years, i.e. a fiscal year can be in 2 tax years if it doesn't start on the 6th of April like the tax year.

The next question I have for you is related to payroll, and it is:

What is a Tax return?

In the United Kingdom, a **tax return** is a document that a business must file with the HM Revenue & Customs declaring liability for taxation. Different bodies (taxpayers) must file separate returns concerning various forms of taxation. The main returns currently in use in the UK are:

- SA100 – This is for individuals paying Income Tax

- SA800 – This one is for partnerships
- SA900 – This is for trusts and estates of deceased persons.
- CT600 - for companies paying Corporation Tax
- P35 – This is for PAYE deductions by employers and National Insurance contributions
- VAT100 for value-added tax (VAT)

Legally, a taxpayer is obliged to submit a tax return when HMRC requests it by sending a notice to file a tax return, either because the taxpayer has registered for self-assessment voluntarily or because HMRC believes one to be required - HMRC can request a tax return from anyone for any reason.

Under UK tax legislation, taxpayers are obliged to notify HMRC when they have a liability to tax no later than nine months and a day after the end of the tax year in which they became liable. Depending on the taxpayer's circumstances and the tax owed, they may do this by registering for self-assessment and completing a tax return.

What is PAYE and when does a business have to register for PAYE?

PAYE means Pay As You Earn and it is a system of paying income tax and national insurance contributions in the UK. Employers deduct tax and national insurance contributions from employees' wages or occupational pension before paying their wages or pension.

A business must register for PAYE scheme when it becomes an employer; that is when it takes in its first employee.

Are you okay so far?

Great! Here is our next question;

What is VAT and when does a business have to register for VAT?

VAT is a tax on consumer spending. VAT-registered businesses add it to the cost of most goods and services supplied in the UK and Isle of Man by and paid by the customer. VAT registered businesses can recover some of the VAT they pay on purchases and expenses.

ACCOUNTING JOB QUESTIONS AND ANSWERS

VAT Registration:

Compulsory registration - You must register for VAT if: your VAT taxable turnover is more than £85,000 (the 'threshold') in 12 months or if you expect to go over the threshold in a single 30-day period.
20% is the current standard rate of VAT in the UK

If you are a VAT registered business, each month or quarter you must produce and reconcile your VAT Return. It's crucial that you submit the correct values to HMRC.

Let's move on. Next question;

What would you say every business is fundamentally involved in doing?

It is the **Buying & Selling of goods/services.**

You see, wherever it operates in the world, every business is fundamentally involved in Buying & selling of goods/services.

Wouldn't you agree?
Pause for a little while and think about it; herein lies, the foundation for you to understand practical accounting.

Let me explain: If businesses did not buy and sell, what would be the need for accountants? Think about it; there would be no need for accountants.

You see, at the heart of accounting in practice is the understanding that buying and selling creates a series of transactions that accountants need to analyse and process and then produce reports summarising the financial performance of the business for a given period.

The reports then are used by the business owners and executive management in making decisions for the successful management of the business.

So, I think at this point, it would be beneficial for us to look at the accounting process for the buying/purchasing and selling process in a business.

We will start by looking at the **Accounts Payable process** – which is the accounting tasks you would need to do if this was your job role.

So, let me ask you in a way that you might be asked in a job interview – see next page.

Describe the Accounts Payable (AP) process?

Here they are:

| Step 1. Raise a purchase order | Step 2. Send the purchse order to the prefered supplier | Step 3. Receive deliveries from the supplier | Step 4. Post the supplier invoice to the purchase ledger | Step 5. Pay supplier asper the agreed days | Step 6. Reconcile supplier statements periodically |

Fig. 1

Let's spend some time exploring the steps mentioned in the figure above

Okay, to begin with, it is essential to know that a business can buy goods & services both in cash and on credit. When it buys on credit, it creates – a payable (which means something purchased on credit and payment will be due at a later date). When it buys in cash, that's different; it has made a cash payment.

Let's look at those steps (see figure 1 above)

Step 1: Raising a purchase order

First, let's define a purchase order. What is it?

Well, a purchase order is a legally binding document between a supplier and a buyer. It details the items the buyer agrees to purchase at a certain price point. It also outlines the delivery/shipping date and terms of payment for the buyer.

Purchase orders are often used when a buyer wants to purchase supplies or inventory on account; this means that the supplier delivers or ships the purchased items before payment, with the purchase order serving as its risk protection.

How should you go about raising a purchase order?

First, a purchase requisition for the details of what needs to be purchased should be raised by the person or department that needs the goods or services. The request should then be sent to the appropriate budget holder(s) for approval.

When the Budget Holder approves the requisition, it should then be sent to the purchasing department, and a Purchase Order will be raised. The order will typically have:
- Purchase Order (PO) number
- Delivery/Shipping date
- Billing address
- Delivery/Shipping address
- Requested terms
- A list of products/services with quantities and price

Step 2: Placing the order with the preferred supplier.

The Purchase Order can then be faxed or emailed to the supplier if necessary.

Orders should not be placed with suppliers until the purchase order has been generated. The purchase order number should be given to the supplier who should in turn quote this number on their invoice.

Step 3: Receiving delivery of goods/services from a supplier

When the supplier delivers the goods, you should then raise a Goods Received Note (GRN). A GRN is a record of goods received at the point of receipt. You should raise the GRN after inspecting delivery for proof of order receipt. It's used by stores, procurement and finance to raise any issues, update your stock records and it should be matched against the original purchase order and supplier invoice, to allow payment to be made.

GRNs play an essential part in the accounts payable process by confirming that items have been received as expected, in accordance with the original purchase order, and that the items can, therefore, be invoiced by the supplier and subsequently paid for by the buyer.

Step 4: Post the invoice from supplier to the purchase ledger

The "Tax Invoice" received from the supplier should now be posted to the accounting software.

An invoice is a document that a business issues to its customers, asking the customers to pay for the goods or services that the business has supplied to them. Invoices can be issued either before or after the goods or services are supplied.

If the business issuing the invoices is registered for VAT, the invoices must comply with specific requirements as laid down by HMRC.

Many accounting software these days are used to raise purchase orders, and they seamlessly allow you to update the records with the supplier invoices received and thus easily record the supplier invoices.

Features of a valid supplier invoice	
Address details	Invoices must be addressed to the business or department within the organisation. The name of an individual may also appear as long as this is an authorised signatory
Status of document	The document must be an invoice rather than a delivery note, order acknowledgement or statement. Some invoices from smaller suppliers may not contain all of the details for VAT purposes. If the word 'invoice' appears on the document, then it should be treated as an invoice.
Accurate	The currency value in the document should be arithmetically correct.
VAT invoice	Invoices that charge VAT must contain all of the following details in addition to those given above: • Supplier VAT number; • Supplier's trading name and address; • Description of goods or services; • Invoice number; • Invoice date; • Time of supply – 'tax point' if different from the invoice date; • Analysis of VAT charged, including value and rate used

Here is an example of an invoice:

Tower Chartered Accountants
25 Canada Square
Canary Wharf, London
E14 5LQ

Invoice Number 000787
Invoice Date: 06/03/20XX
VAT No. 123456789

Invoice to:
Kilmorie Capital Ltd
22 Firs Road, London
SE23 1BB

Qty	Description	Rate	Net Amount
1	Yearend accounts preparation	1,500.00	1,500.00
1	Payroll services	250.00	250.00
		Subtotal	1,750.00
		Tax @20%	350.00
		Total Amount Payabble	2,100.00

Step 5: Pay the supplier as per the agreed days

Just as you expect others to pay you on time, it's just as important that you pay your bills on time.

A supplier invoice should ideally not be paid without a matching purchase order (except for utility bills like gas, electricity, telephone – which generally might be paid by direct debit/standing order). This ensures both that the organisation does not pay for unauthorised purchases and that authorised purchases will be paid in a timely fashion.

Suppose that today is the end of the month, and you have to pay for 200 invoices from 50 suppliers. You can process each payment individually by going into the supplier accounts - select the invoices, generate the payment list, write out the cheques, get the manager to authorise, send the cheques to the suppliers together with remittance advise notes.

This process will probably take you hours to complete manually.

There could be a better way.

If your purchase ledger system has a Batch Payments to Suppliers facility, all this is going to take you is the best part of 10 minutes. Just display a list of the 200 invoices on the screen, scan through them to note down the ones you don't want to pay, press the Select All button to highlight the lot, double-click on the two or more invoices you want to deselect, then press the button.

Here is how you go about it in detail; typically, the process will involve several stages, with the opportunity to review and correct at each stage. Below is a step by step example of how you might want to handle a batch payment run:

1. *Print a report of invoices due for payment and send this report to the manager requesting authorisation to pay.*
2. *Manager returns report indicating invoices approved or refused.*
3. *Display the list of all invoices due for payment on the Accounts software on-screen, press select to highlight all invoices and then deselect any invoices that have not been authorised for payment.*
4. *Print off resultant remittance advice note(s) in the draft to check for errors. Any necessary corrections should be done. Use the software to recalculate payments and reprint remittances.*
5. *Check and reprint until satisfied and then finalise the payment. Many Accounts packages allocate reference numbers to each payment. [Note - Payment transactions are now committed and cannot be changed]*
6. *The software prints final remittance advice and outputs BACS file, output onto an external disk.*
7. *Load file from external disk into your banks BACS system and complete the process.*

Batch Payments to Suppliers is one of the biggest time-savers in any accounts package, and it is handy if you process many payments at one time. However, if you only issue a dozen or so payments, you might as well keep doing them manually.

Send suppliers remittance advice slips

A remittance advice note is a note sent from a customer to his supplier, informing the supplier that he/she has paid the invoice. The advice may contain elements such as a text note, the invoice number and the invoice amount, among others.

Remittance advice notes are not required, but they are seen as a courtesy since they make it easier for the supplier to match invoices with payments.

Remittance advice note could be compared to a receipt from a cash register, in that they serve as a record of received payment.

At its simplest, a remittance advice note can be a letter or a note that outlines the invoice number and the payment amount sent or enclosed (such as when attached to a cheque).

Send your suppliers' remittance advice notes. It's a courteous business practice.

Step 6: Supplier statement reconciliation

Most organisations have to reconcile supplier accounts as part of their audit processes, which is an arduous task.

In principle, the process for reconciling supplier accounts is very straightforward. The supplier's credit control department sends a statement of account, which contains the unpaid invoices on their sales ledger, to the buyer's accounts payable department. The accounts payable team at the buyer's organisation compare the statement to their accounts payable in the creditors' ledger should be immediately debited. However, the money might not arrive at the supplier's account for a few days (especially if you are paying by cheque). In the meantime, the supplier will be showing that amount still owing, and the supplier thus will send you a statement showing unpaid invoices.

When you receive a supplier's statement, you should try to reconcile it to the supplier's account in your creditors' ledger. The term 'reconcile' means that you try to explain the difference between the two figures.

Any differences that you cannot explain are probably caused by errors – either yours or the suppliers.

To reconcile a supplier's statement to the balance on an account, you must go through the entries on each, marking off the ones which match. Any entries which don't match, whether on the statement or the account, need to be investigated and explained.

The first stage in the reconciliation is to 'tick off' all the items in common between the account and the statement. These items cannot be contributing to the difference. Whatever is left unticked should be "investigated."

Generally, to reconcile the supplier's statement, adjust for any payments made on or before the reconciliation date. For the ledger account, add any invoices issued by the supplier on or before the reconciliation date, but not yet entered into the supplier's account.

Supplier statement reconciliation is an opportunity for accounts payable to spot any discrepancies before suppliers request for payment of unpaid invoices is processed and to make sure the invoice process is complete.

The key to identifying discrepancies is to determine which invoices or credit notes on the supplier statement that are not on the accounts payable ledger or vice versa.

We are going to look at credit notes next.

What is a Credit note?

A credit note is effectively a negative invoice - it's a way of showing a customer that they don't have to pay the full amount of an invoice.

A credit note might either cancel an invoice out entirely if it's for the same amount as the invoice or cancel it for just the amount on the credit note if it is for less than the invoice.

A credit note can be issued to correct a mistake if the invoice has been overstated or to reimburse the buyer entirely if the goods have been returned. Credit notes are only issued where products or services have been bought or sold on credit. If a cash transaction was the case, a refund usually is what the affected party (customer or supplier) receives.

Supplier credit notes

If you return goods to a supplier for full or partial credit, the supplier should ideally issue you a credit note that you can use to adjust your accounts accordingly.

If you have paid the invoice before the goods arrive and then have to return them due to damage or unsuitability, then a credit note can be issued.

If you intend to buy more from that supplier, the credit can be offset against future purchases which in some cases would be the supplier's preference or you may require a refund of your payment.

We have so far established that business buy and sell goods/services, and, we have just looked at the Accounts Payable – the buying process and how to account for it. Let's also look at the sales process and how to account for it – the Accounts Receivable

Describe the Accounts Receivable (AR) process?

Here they are:

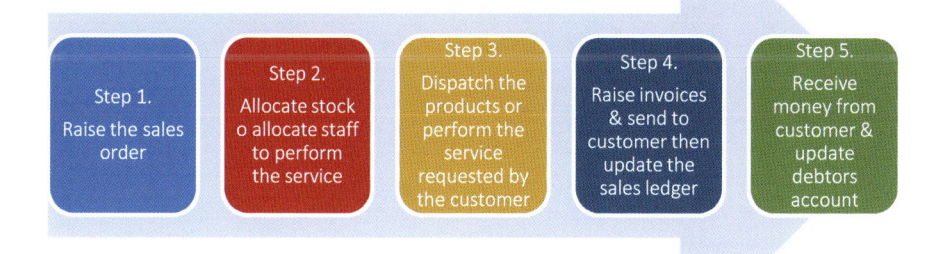

| Step 1. Raise the sales order | Step 2. Allocate stock o allocate staff to perform the service | Step 3. Dispatch the products or perform the service requested by the customer | Step 4. Raise invoices & send to customer then update the sales ledger | Step 5. Receive money from customer & update debtors account |

Fig. 2

You see, when a business is involved in selling its products or services, it can do so by selling on credit (this results in what is called Receivables) or selling in cash (this results in what is called technically called in accounting receipts) or you can sell in both ways (and most businesses do it both ways).

Accounting for the sales made on credit is carried out in a series of tasks/procedures called the Accounts receivable process as illustrated in figure 2.

What does 'on credit' mean? Well, it means when you sell a service or item to a customer and are not paid immediately - you are extending credit to them.

So, the accounts receivable process does not apply to sales where you are paid immediately. Sales, where you are paid promptly, are called cash sales or receipts, and their accounting process is a bit different and quite straightforward.

Now, let's look at the **Accounts receivable process** – as illustrated in figure 2 above and understand the steps involved in the process in a bit more detail.

Step 1. Send quotation for your goods/service(s) to the customer

What's a quotation/quote? Well, a quotation or quote in accounting is a formal document which explains a business's pricing for a product or service and gives the customer a precise cost for the product/service.
When a customer asks you for a quote, it means they're seriously considering doing business with you. All your sales and marketing efforts have paid off! You've shown that your service has value, and you're one step away from closing the deal.

Quotations usually are given to customers by sales staff, but the quotation stage is a significant and integral part of the accounts receivable process/function because once accepted by the customer, it has legal status in many countries. So, you usually can't charge more (raise an invoice for a different value - higher) for the product/work than you've quoted.

Step 2: Receive & process customer orders

Once the customer is happy with the quotation, they usually send an order – purchase order (ask for a written one, not verbal and make a note of the purchase order number from the customer) for the goods/services your company has quoted for them.
Your task then is to process that purchase order from the customer by raising a sales order.

A sales order is an internal document of your company, your company itself generates it.

Your sales order should record the customer's originating purchase order which is an external document. Rather than using the customer's purchase order document, an internal sales order form allows the internal audit control of completeness to be monitored as a sequential sales order number can be used by your company for its sales order documents.

The customer's Purchase Order (PO) is the originating document which triggers the creation of the sales order, and a sales order, being an internal document, can, therefore, contain many customer purchase orders under it.

If your business is in a manufacturing environment, a sales order can be converted into a work order to show that work is about to begin to manufacture, build or engineer the products the customer wants.

Many computerised accounting software systems now have the function of sales order processing built in, and hopefully, these should not be a tough task for you.

Step 3&4: Deliver the goods/services to the customer and raise the invoice

Having converted the order from the customer to accounts receivable, you will have to deliver the goods or perform the service(s) as per the request from the customer.

Bear in mind that the invoice you raise for the product or service delivered to your customer is a legal, financial document of which you have to keep records by law.

Therefore, when raising a Sales Invoice, the following should be noted:

- Your business name and address details should be in the invoice
- A unique invoice reference/number that will relate to this invoice only.
- A date for the invoice (which will generally be the date on which the invoice is created/raised)
- The prices and goods/service described in the invoice should be those agreed with the customer (via the quotation step discussed above)
- Invoices should be sent out as soon as possible following the supply of goods/services and no later than "X" number of days after the supply (These depends on what your company policy is)
- Additions and calculations in the invoice should always be checked before invoices are dispatched to customers.
- A total amount for the invoice.
- The payment terms for the invoice (i.e., how long the customer has to pay)
- If you are a registered Limited company, you must include Your Company Number and your full registered company address on the invoice.

Addressing a sales invoice

Correctly addressing invoices is crucial. If an error is made, it may be impossible to collect the outstanding debt from the customer.

The following steps should be taken:
- ✓ Find out who exactly will be making the payment from the customer's side.
- ✓ Invoices should be addressed as follows:

> *for the attention of:*
> ABC PLC/LTD
> *Company's full address*

- ✓ Customer Purchase Order Number - so they know which purchase order the invoice relates to if they are using an order management system.
- ✓ Details on how to pay, including bank account details for BACs/ online payments.
- ✓ If you are VAT registered you must also include: The amount of VAT on each line of the invoice and the VAT rate charged OR the total amount of VAT charged on the invoice, and the rate, if VAT applies to all items on the invoice and don't forget to include your VAT number on the invoice.

Step 5: Maintaining invoices & payments

This is the core of your accounts receivable procedures. There is no point in selling to customers on credit and failing to collect the outstanding amounts later.

Here are the steps to follow from the time you give the customer their invoice:-

If you are using a Manual Receivables System (MRS)

a. Print a copy of the invoices and place it into your *Receivables file in sequential order - either by date or invoice number.
b. Make a cover page on which to list the unpaid invoices. Draw up columns to display i) the date, ii) the customer name, iii) the invoice number, iv) the amount, v) paid date. Keep this cover page in the front of the folder.
c. When payment is received, either by cash, cheque or internet banking, write the date it was paid into the 'paid date' column of the Receivables cover page. You can also make a note (hand-written or stamped) of the date paid on the invoice itself.
d. Remove the invoice from the Receivables file and place it into a *Sales Invoice file (an archive for all the paid invoices).

*You could instead have one folder with two sections i) Unpaid Invoices, ii) Paid Invoices, this is just one method. You can change it to suit your requirements, and indeed, design a whole different system, as long as what you do helps you keep a handle on those unpaid invoices.

If you are using Computerised Bookkeeping System (CBS)

If you are using bookkeeping software that has a receivables option, it is easy to check what is due, because when you run a receivables report it will only list the invoices that have not been paid – as long as all the payments received have been entered into the program!

Therefore, you do not need to keep a separate receivables folder. You can just place all invoices directly into the Sales Invoices folder because you will use the bookkeeping program for the accounts receivable procedures.

Customer/Debtor credit notes

On the other hand, if a customer returns goods to you for full or partial credit, you should issue the customer with a credit note. The amount shown on the credit note should be equal to the amount of error or overcharge identified. All credit notes are to be raised by the Accounts Receivable team.
Invoices raised to correct an undercharge should refer to the original invoice number.

Financial documents

The result of buying and selling will generate financial documents such as:

- ✓ Invoices
- ✓ Receipts
- ✓ Credit notes
- ✓ Bank statements
- ✓ Contracts, etc.

These financial documents are then used to produce financial reports.

How do you produce financial reports from financial documents?

You can do so by following the three stages shown in the figure on the next page.

This space is for notes

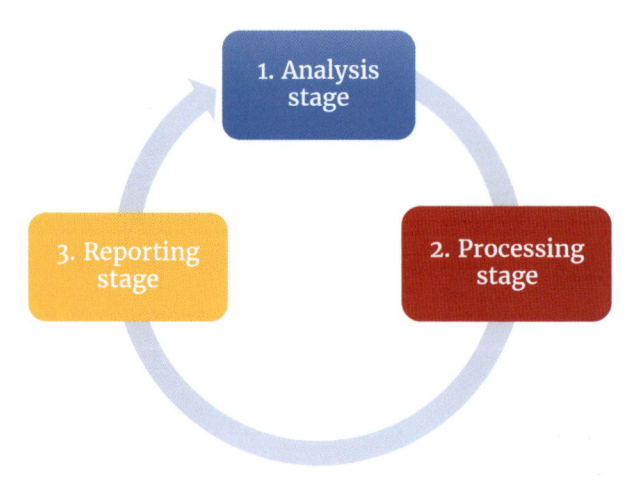

```
         1. Analysis
           stage

3. Reporting      2. Processing
    stage             stage
```

Fig. 3

Let's look at each of these stages in a bit more detail. Shall we?

Let's begin with the 1st stage - **Analysis stage.**

There are three things to do in the analysis stage – see next page.

1. Classification	2. Valuation	3. Timing
• Customer/supplier codes • Nominal code • Product code • Tax code • Department code	• Checking the accuracy of values in the financial documents	• Making sure that the financial documents are processed in the correct financial year

i. *Classification of financial documents* is accomplished through coding. That is: writing down the Customer/Supplier codes on to the invoices, listing the appropriate nominal codes in the financial records for the goods or services bought or sold, selecting the correct product codes, using the appropriate tax codes for the VAT rate used in the financial documents and if applicable the departmental codes for the department to allocate the expense.

ii. The other thing you will be doing during the analysis stage is Valuation; that is checking the accuracy of the values in the financial documents, and

iii. lastly, you will also need to make sure that the financial records you intend to process are within the fiscal year you are dealing with currently. Right timing.

Ultimately, the integrity and accuracy of the resulting financial reports are mostly based on the result of this stage. It is therefore vital that financial documents be correctly analysed before moving them into the next stage – Processing stage.

2nd stage: Processing stage.

Is mostly about data entry

Using double entry bookkeeping principle

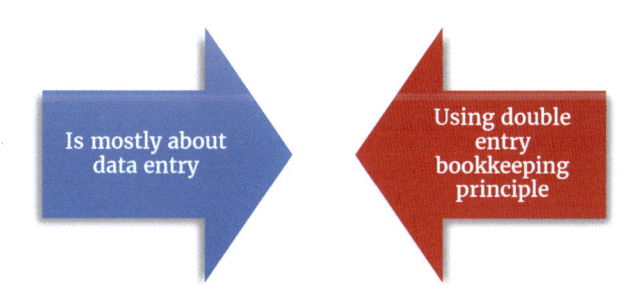

Fig. 4

The processing stage also known as the recording stage is mostly about data entry (of all the financial documents that have been analysed) are then recorded in the general ledger using the double-entry bookkeeping principle.

Double entry simply states that:

For every debit entry

There is an equal & corresponding credit entry

These entries are recorded in the general ledger accounts

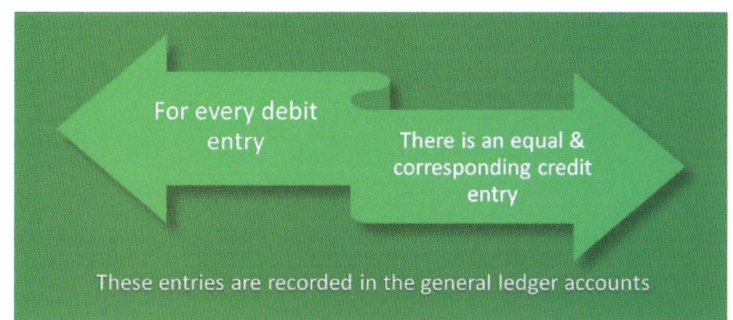

Fig. 5

Double entry will require that a debit and credit entry be made in two separate ledger accounts for one financial transaction.

Double-entry accounting takes advantage of the accounting equation: Assets = Liabilities + Owners Equity. The recording of assets, liabilities and shareholders' equity allows you to prepare a balance sheet.

There are five major classes of general ledger accounts

P	PURCHASES	These class of ledger accounts have debit balances in the general ledger.
E	EXPENSES	
A	ASSETS	A debit entry would increase the balance in these class of accounts, and a credit entry would decrease the balance in these class of account
R	REVENUE	These class of ledger accounts have credit balances in the general ledger.
L	LIABILITIES	A credit entry would increase the balance in these class of accounts, and a debit entry would decrease the balance in these class of account

PEARL is an acronym for the five main classes of accounts: **P**urchases, **E**xpenses, **A**ssets, **R**evenue and **L**iability accounts.

Another way of looking at the "behaviour" of general ledger accounts is using the acronym: DEAD CLIC

The DEAD part of the acronym means;
Accounts with Debit (D) balances in the ledgers are (E) Expense accounts (e.g., rent), (A) Asset accounts (e.g., Cash), (D)Drawings account (withdrawals by the owner). The balances in these accounts increase by debit entries and decrease by credit entries.

For example, a cash payment of electricity bill has the following impact:
The value of expense made (a cost of the business - electricity) will increase – thus a debit entry in that expense account (the electricity account), and the balance of cash (asset) will now decrease – hence a credit entry in the cash account.

On the other side, the CLIC side of the acronym means; accounts with (C) Credit balances are: (L)Liability accounts (e.g., Loan account), (I) Income accounts (e.g., Sales revenue account) and (C) Capital accounts (e.g., Share capital account) have credit balances in the ledgers by default.

To increase the balance in any of these accounts, you do so by a credit entry, and you decrease their balances by debit entries.

For example, getting a low-interest loan to clear a high-interest business credit card bill will have the following effect:

The balance in the liability account (Company Credit card) will reduce – thus a debit entry, and the balance in the yet another Liability account (bank loan account) will increase – thus a credit entry.

Look at the summary of an illustration of DEAD CLIC in figure 6 on the next page.

Accounts with Debit balances.
(These accounts increase by debit entries & decrease by credit entries)

- Expense accounts
- Asset accounts
- Drawings account

Accounts with Credit balances
(These accounts increase by credit entries & decrease by debit entries)

- Liability accounts
- Income accounts
- Capital accounts

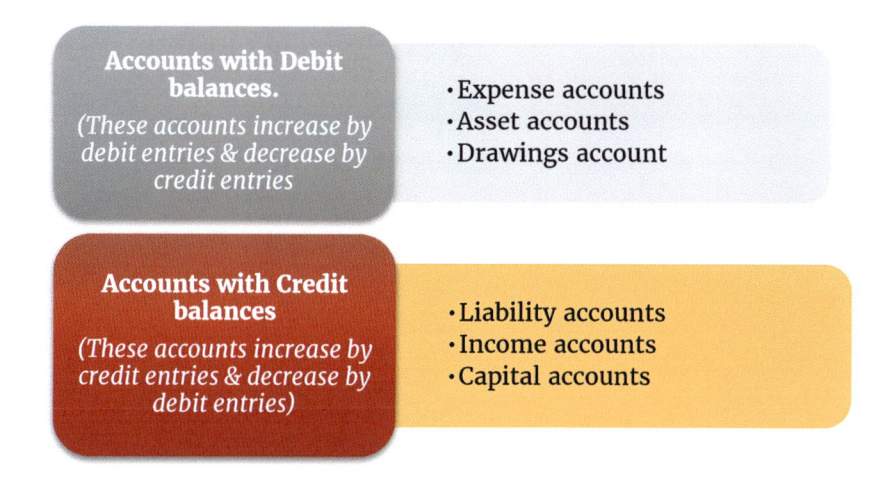

Fig. 6

Now, moving on, the processing of transactions from the analysed documents as seen in stage 1 and two above is all about maintaining the fundamental accounting equation.

The fundamental accounting equation states that:

Assets = Liabilities + Owners Equity

Fig. 7

This accounting equation is also sometimes represented as;
Assets-Liabilities = Owners Equity and the technical accounting term for this equation is the ***Balance Sheet***.

So far, we have looked at two stages of practical accounting: see figure 8

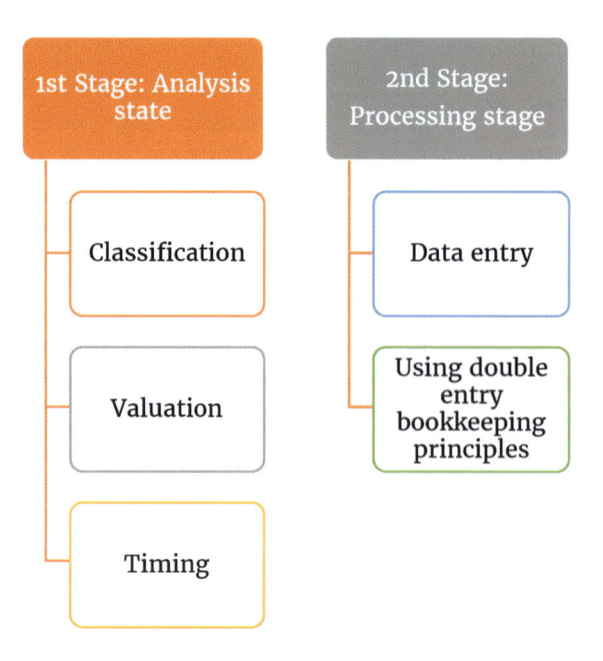

1st Stage: Analysis state
- Classification
- Valuation
- Timing

2nd Stage: Processing stage
- Data entry
- Using double entry bookkeeping principles

Fig. 8

The 3rd stage is the reporting stage, and this stage ultimately involves the production of financial reports such as:

- ✓ Statement of financial position (Balance sheet)
- ✓ Statement of comprehensive income (Profit and loss account)
- ✓ Other financial statements like cash flow statement, management account reports, etc.

The Finance manager mostly does the report production stage unless you work in a tiny company where you are the sole accountant then you will do both the analysis and processing stage as well as the reporting stage.

Like the other two preceding stages, there are three significant things to do at this stage as well, and they are:

i. Nominal error checks and corrections,
ii. making period end/yearend adjustments and
iii. producing period end/year-end reports.

See the illustrative diagram, figure 9 below.

3rd stage: The Reporting stage

Step 1:	Step 2:	Step 3:
Check the general ledger account for errors and correct them	Perform period end/yearend adjustments	Produce accounting reports

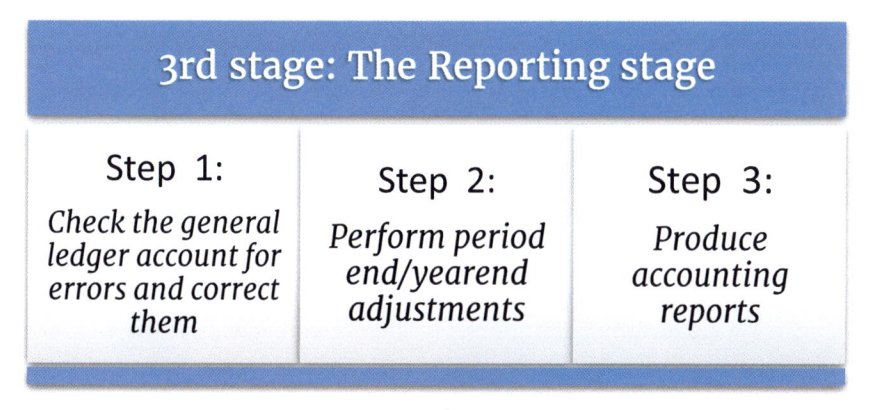

Fig. 9

Let's look at each of the three steps in the above figure in a little bit more detail.

1. Check general ledger accounts for errors & correcting them	2. perform period end adjustments & reconciliations	3. Produce accounting reports
• Produce the trial balance
• Check each general ledger account in the trial balance to make sure there are no mistakes in it
• Any mistakes discovered should be corrected	• Accruals & prepayment adjustements
• Bank reconciliations
• Balance sheet reconciliations
• Debtors & creditors reconciliations
• VAT & Wages reconciliations	• Statement of comprehensive income
• Statement of financial position
• Management account reports
• Cash flow statement
• Ratio analysis report.

Fig. 10

Let's begin with the checking of the general ledger accounts for error & correcting those errors.

When doing the nominal error checks and corrections, it's best if you produce a trial balance first.

You should then check each nominal account in the trial balance for any errors (errors of omission, commission, errors of principle and arithmetic errors)

Any errors discovered should then be corrected.

After checking and correcting any general ledger account errors, you should then proceed and make period end/yearend adjustments. That is; dealing with things such as Accruals & prepayments, Depreciation, control account reconciliations (Debtors, Creditors, VAT, Wages), Capital allowances calculations and doing bank reconciliations for the period/year.

Once the period end/year end procedures and adjustments have been done, you are now ready to produce the period end/year-end reports, and you should proceed to do so. The statements you will generate will include: Balance sheet, Profit and loss account and other reports that management will deem necessary to provide such as management accounts report.

At this point, you will also have enough information to be able to produce and file the Corporation tax return, and Companies house abridged accounts if you are at the year-end.

Let's sum up what we have been talking about so far by looking at what I call the accounting cycle wheel. It is a snapshot of how accounting is done in practice.

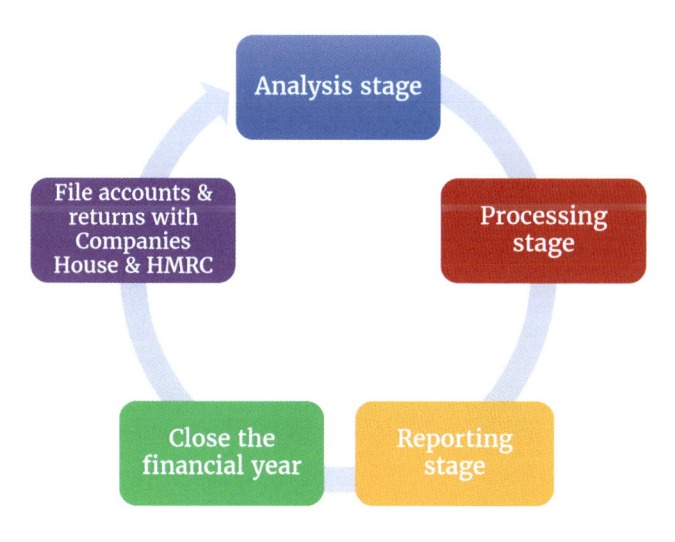

Fig. 11

We began by looking at the Analysis stage: That is; doing Classification - ensuring that the values in the financial documents are correct and that they have dates that relate to the current fiscal year.
After that, we moved to the Processing/Recording stage – Here you process/record the transactions in the financial documents using double entry principles.

After that, we enter the reporting stage, and in here you begin by checking for errors in the general ledger accounts used, correcting any identified errors and making adjustments in the general ledger and then producing period end and reports.

After you've successfully done all the three stages, you should then close the financial year, produce the statutory accounts & returns and then submit those accounts and returns to HMRC and Companies House.

Are you okay up to this point so far?

Great!

Moving on, here is another question for you;

Whose responsibility is it to submit annual accounts to government authorities?

That would be the Director(s) of the company.

You have done well so far, let's now wrap this up by looking at the two primary financial statements.

How do you present the two primary financial statements?

The Statement of Comprehensive Income (Income statement or Profit & Loss account) and the Statement of Financial Position (Balance sheet) are the two common financial statements.

Let's look at the Income Statement and what the prescribed format of its preparation is according to the International Accounting Standard 1 (IAS 1 - Presentation of Financial Statements).

This space is for notes

XYZ Income statement
For the period ended DD/MM/YYYY

	Notes	£ Current Year	£ Prior Year
Revenue	1	X	X
Cost of Sales	2	X	X
Gross profit		XX	XX
Other income	3	X	X
Distribution cost	4		
Administration expenses	5	X	X
Other expenses	6	X	X
Finance charges	7	X	X
Profit before tax		XX	XX
Tax	8	X	X
Profit after tax		XX	XX

The income statement as you have probably noticed has headings on the left-hand side. I want us to explore those headings to understand what can be recorded under each.

Revenue
Revenue includes income you have earned from the principal activities of your business. So, for example, if your business manufacturers & sells electronic appliances, revenue will comprise of the sales from the electronic appliance business. Conversely, if in the same manufacturing business you earn interest on your bank account, it shall not be classified as revenue but as other income.

Cost of Sales
Cost of sales represents the cost of goods sold or services rendered during the accounting period in your business.

For example, for a retailer, the cost of sales will be the sum of inventory at the start of the period and purchases during the period minus any closing stock.

In case of a manufacturer, however, cost of sales will also include production costs incurred in the manufacture of goods during a period such as the cost of direct labour, direct material consumption, depreciation of plant and machinery and factory overheads, etc.

Other Income
Other income consists of income earned from activities that are not related to the primary business of your company. For example, other income in the case of a manufacturer of electronic appliances may include:
- Gain on disposal of fixed assets
- Interest income on bank deposits
- Exchange gain on translation of a foreign currency bank account

Distribution Cost
Distribution cost includes expenses incurred in delivering goods from the business premises to customers.

Administrative Expenses
Administrative expenses generally comprise of costs relating to the management and support functions within an organisation which are not directly involved in the production and supply of goods and services offered by the entity.

Examples of administrative expenses include:
- Gross Wages
- Rent & Rates
- Heat, Light and Power
- Motor Expenses
- Travelling & Entertainment
- Printing & Stationery
- Telephone & Computer charges
- Professional Fees
- Equipment Hire & Rental
- Maintenance
- Bank Charges & Interest
- Depreciation
- Bad Debts
- General Expenses

Finance Charges

Finance charges usually comprise of interest expense on loans and debentures.
The effect of present value adjustments of discounted provisions are also included in finance charges (e.g. unwinding of discount on provision for decommissioning cost).

Tax

Income tax expense recognised during a period is generally comprised of the following four elements:
- Current period's estimated tax charge
- Marginal rate relief for small companies with a profit of between £300,000 & £1.5M.
- Prior period tax adjustments
- Deferred tax expense

Prior Period Comparatives
Prior period financial information is presented alongside the current period's financial results to facilitate comparison of performance over the periods.

It is therefore essential that prior period comparative figures presented in the income statement relate to a similar period.

For example, if you are preparing an income statement for the six months ending 31 December 20X1, comparative figures of the prior period should relate to the six months ending 31 December 20XX.

This space is for notes

The format of a simple management account profit & Loss statement

	Notes	Current Year		Prior Year	
SALES/REVENUE	1				
Product Sales		X		X	
Export Sales		X		X	
Sales of Assets		X		X	
Credit charges		X		X	
Other sales		X		X	
Total Sales (A)			XX		XX
PURCHASES (Cost of Sales)	2				
Purchases		X		X	
Purchase charges		X		X	
Stock		X		X	
Total Cost of Sales (B)			XX		XX
OVERHEADS	3				
Gross Wages		X		X	
Rent & Rates		X		X	
Heat, Light and Power		X		X	
Motor Expenses		X		X	
Travelling & Entertainment		X		X	
Printing & Stationery		X		X	
Telephone & Computer charges		X		X	
Professional Fees		X		X	
Equipment Hire & Rental		X		X	
Maintenance		X		X	
Bank Charges & Interest		X		X	
Depreciation		X		X	
Bad Debts		X		X	
General Expenses		X		X	
Total Overheads (C)			XX		XX
Net Profit/(Loss) Before Taxation (D)		A-(B+C)	XX		XX
Taxation	4	E	X		X
Net Profit/(Loss) After Taxation		D-E	XX		XX

That's about it for now with the income statement.

ACCOUNTING JOB QUESTIONS AND ANSWERS

Let's move onto the format of the Balance sheet. See next page.

XYZ BALANCE SHEET:
As at DD/MM/YYYY

	Notes	Current Year	Prior Year
ASSETS			
Non-Current Assets			
Property, Plant & Equipment	5	x	x
Goodwill	6	x	x
Intangible assets	7	x	x
Total non-current assets		xx	xx
Current Assets			
Inventories	8	x	x
Trade receivables	9	x	x
Cash & Cash equivalents	10	x	x
Total current assets		xx	xx
LIABILITIES			
Current Liabilities			
Trade & other payables	11	x	x
Short-term borrowings	12	x	x
Current portion of long-term borrowings	13	x	x
Total current liabilities		xx	xx
Current assets less current Liabilities		xx	xx
TOTAL ASSETS		xx	xx
Non-current Liabilities			
Long-term borrowings	14	x	x
Corporation tax	4	x	x
Total non-current liabilities		xx	xx
Net Assets (Total Assets less total liabilities) – (A)		xx	xx
CAPITAL & RESERVES			
Share capital	15	x	x
Retained earnings	16	x	x
Revaluation reserve	17	x	x
Total Capital & Reserves (B)		xx	xx

Just as we looked at the "components" of the income statement, let's do the same with the Balance sheet.
The statement of Financial Position, also known as the Balance Sheet is comprised of the following three elements:

ASSETS:
As a way of definition, an asset is a resource that an entity owns or controls to derive economic benefits from its use.

Assets must be classified in the balance sheet as current or noncurrent depending on the duration over which an entity expects to derive economic benefit from its use.

An asset which will deliver economic benefits to the entity over the long term is classified as non-current whereas those assets that are expected to be realised within one year from the reporting date are classified as current assets.

Assets are also classified in the statement of financial position by their nature:

Tangible & intangible - Non-current assets with physical substance (Tangible) are classified as property, plant and equipment whereas assets without any physical substance are classified as intangible assets. Goodwill is a type of intangible asset.

Inventories balance - includes goods that are held for sale in the ordinary course of the business. Inventories may include raw materials, finished goods and work in progress.

Trade receivables - include the amounts that are recoverable from customers upon credit sales. Trade receivables are presented in the statement of financial position after the deduction of allowance for bad debts.

Cash and cash equivalents - include cash in hand along with any short-term investments that are readily convertible into known amounts of cash. Liabilities:

LIABILITIES:
A liability is an obligation that a business owes to someone, and its settlement involves the transfer of cash or other resources. Liabilities must be classified in the statement of financial position as current or non-current depending on the duration over which the entity intends to settle the liability.

A liability which will be settled over the long term is classified as noncurrent or long-term whereas those liabilities that are expected to be settled within one year from the reporting date are classified as current liabilities.

Liabilities are also classified in the statement of financial position by their nature:

Trade and other payables - primarily include liabilities due to suppliers and contractors for credit purchases. Sundry payables which are too insignificant to be presented separately on the face of the statement of financial position are also classified in this category.

Short-term borrowings - typically include bank overdrafts and short-term bank loans with a repayment schedule of fewer than 12 months.

Long-term borrowings - comprise of loans which are to be repaid over a period that exceeds one year. Current portion of long-term borrowings include the instalments of long-term borrowings that are due within one year of the reporting date. ***Current Tax Payable*** - is usually presented as a separate line item in the statement of financial position due to the materiality of the amount.

EQUITY:
Equity is what the business owes to its owners. Equity is derived by deducting total liabilities from the total assets. It, therefore, represents the residual interest in the business that belongs to the owners.

Equity is usually presented in the statement of financial position under the following categories:

Share capital - this represents the amount invested by the owners in the entity

Retained earnings - comprises the total net profit or loss retained in the business after distribution to the owners in the form of dividends.
Revaluation reserve - contains the net surplus of any upward and downward revaluation of property, plant and equipment recognised directly in equity. That is it about the statement of financial position that we will so far cover in this book.

"Serve others. That is the secret to greatness, friendships and money – lots of it"

Sterling Libs

*"In life, you never know when opportunity strikes. Best to be always prepared. And how do you do that? By knowing your craft or subject in and out. **Your** Opportunity will often strike within your area of expertise."*
Sterling Libs

HOW DO YOU ANSWER TRICKY TECHNICAL JOB INTERVIEW QUESTIONS?

If you were invited to a job interview and were asked why you should be hired over someone else or if you have an accounting job already, but you want a promotion and you were asked why you should be promoted over someone else, how would you answer that question?

There is no straightforward answer to this question.

What you need to consider is your skill set together with your experience (if any) and how that helps you add value to the organisation.

You should also be very articulate and confident when answering these kinds of questions and give concrete examples of how you will be the perfect fit for the role. Make sure you have done thorough research on the role and the company and be very prepared to answer any questions that may arise related to the role and your competencies for it.

What is the difference between accounts receivable (AR) and accounts payable (AP)?

Recruiters use this accounting job interview question to find out more about the general accounting knowledge of entry-level job candidates for bookkeeping or accounting clerk openings.

Your responses, both verbal and non-verbal, will reveal whether you understand accounting fundamentals which the recruiter is actually looking for from you. Make sure you have a thorough understanding and application of what the accounts payable and accounts receivable processes are.

When a company is using double-entry accounting, what elements of a given ledger must be equal?"

As with the previous question, the manner in which you reply this question may show the recruiter whether you are under- or overqualified for a junior-level job at their company. Measure out your answer here accordingly.

If a company has three bank accounts for processing payments, what is the minimum number of ledgers it needs?

A recruiter will use this kind of question to explore your knowledge of ledgers. Your response will most likely reveal to the recruiter the extent to which you have thought through how accounts relate to lines of business and generally accepted accounting principles.

What methods have you used for estimating bad debt?

This accounting interview question can open a conversation about the ways you have approached this routine process with previous employers. Your answer will reveal the level of understanding of the methods most commonly used and could open a dialogue about how the recruiter's company handles this.

Which enterprise resource planning (ERP) systems have you used?

If you have experience working for medium to large organisations, you should have an answer for this. A response might include any of the following: Hyperion, Microsoft Dynamics GP or Oracle Enterprise Manager, JD Edwards.

If you are just starting out in your accounting career, you might turn this into a discussion of accounting certifications and future training possibilities. For example, ask which ERP systems they would like you to master.

The discussions you will have with the recruiter about these tools, how you learned them and put them to work, and what applications the recruiter's company uses will reveal how much if any, training might be needed.

What is your experience with developing business metrics?

This interview question can elicit answers useful in evaluating entry-level business or financial analyst candidates all the way up to mid-career professionals who aspire to roles that come with budget and staff oversight responsibilities.

Make sure you are fully prepared and give a confident, concise answer with relevant examples.

If a private company with break-even operations received a £5 million investment, how would you develop a strategy to spend or invest that money?

This is one of those interview questions for accounting that falls into the category of situational interview techniques, a tactic useful in gauging an applicant's ability to think through a scenario like one that might be faced in a more senior finance role.

The answers you give to this kind of questions will show the recruiter if the approach is in alignment with that of their existing team, which will also indicate if you are an excellent fit to their organisation's culture.

What challenges have you faced in leading a team through an analysis project?

This question is designed for probing leadership skills, somewhat general. It is another interview question a recruiter can modify to explore the particularities of their opening or your background better. As with the question above, the answers will reveal the levels of critical thinking skills and elicit a better picture of your leadership techniques.

I also found the following details from indeed really useful, and I would like to pass them on to you. You can find details at *https://www.indeed.com/hire/interview-questions/accountant*

7 Accountant Interview Questions and Answers

Which accounting platforms have you worked with?

Experienced accountants often have worked with multiple accounting applications or enterprise resource planning systems. This question allows the applicant to show their familiarity with prominent accounting and business software packages. Look for answers that include the name and version of the software, as well as the features the applicant is most familiar with. What to look for in an answer:

- Familiarity with prominent software packages
- Understanding of how to use basic features
- Willingness to learn new platforms

Example: "I used QuickBooks when I worked at a small business and Microsoft Dynamics GP at larger enterprises. I'm most familiar with QuickBooks Online and helped my previous employer track and categorise their expenses and invoices.
How have you used automation or workflow streamlining to improve your accounting processes at previous jobs?

How have you used automation or workflow streamlining to improve your accounting processes at previous jobs?

Experienced accountants learn how to do their jobs more efficiently by using advanced tools or software features. The applicant reveals whether they try to look for ways to continually improve their processes and how to use tools to accomplish this goal. What to look for in an answer:

- Creative thinking
- Understanding of accounting business processes
- Strong skills in the accounting solution

Example: "I synchronised the business bank accounts and corporate credit card statements with our accounting solution to decrease how much I had to type manually. I used the extra time to look into accounting discrepancies and follow up with employee expense reports."

What do you do when you have a tight deadline and multiple accounting projects to finish?

Many accounting projects have a strict deadline, and accountants may be working on more than one at a time. This important question gives you insight into how the job seeker prioritises tasks and responds to high-pressure situations. What to look for in an answer:

- Time management techniques for quickly and accurately entering transactions
- Good prioritisation for focusing on the most important accounting duties
- Multitasking for completing different types of reports at the same time

Example: "*I would focus on the most time-sensitive tasks first, as well as those that other people depend on to move forward on the project. If I needed additional resources to remain on schedule, I would ask the appropriate department.*"

How do you answer questions from clients who don't have any background in accounting?

Accountants may need to explain processes or concepts to other people in your organisation who don't know anything about accounting. Look for a response that conveys a willingness to simplify complex information and present it in an easy-to-understand fashion. What to look for in an answer:

- Teaching skills
- Fundamental understanding of accounting concepts
- Patience

Example: "*I would use analogies to help the person understand the information that I'm trying to convey. I wouldn't use any terminology that's accounting-specific, as that would make it difficult for this person to follow along. I spent a lot of time talking to the software development team about what the accounting team needed in our applications. I framed everything in technology terms, such as referring to a general ledger as a database.*"

What strategies do you use to detect fraudulent entries in a journal or ledger?

Accountants need to remain vigilant in fraud detection to protect the company's finances and values. The applicant should have familiarity in using a combination of software features and their own judgment to identify unusual or fraudulent patterns. What to look for in an answer:

- Understanding of common fraudulent behaviour
- Familiarity with fraud monitoring tools
- Appropriate ethics

Example: "*I use proactive monitoring features in the enterprise resource planning platform I use, alongside manual spot checks. The automated monitoring catches errors and anomalies* that may indicate fraud. I conduct a thorough investigation and double-check the numbers to discover what happened.

How do you maintain accounting accuracy?

A small mistake could cost your organisation much money, especially if it goes undetected. Applicants should have several ways to check the accuracy of their accounting, as well as know what to do if they make a mistake. What to look for in an answer:

- Detail-oriented mindset
- Ability to recognise and address errors
- Dedication to accuracy

Example: "I use every tool and resource available to check my work and limit the potential for an error to slip by. At my last job, employees used Expensify to track receipts when they went on business trips. I looked at the real-time reports and compared them to the credit card statements to confirm the numbers. When errors do happen, I address them quickly to limit the damage it could cause."

How have you helped companies or clients save money or better use their available financial resources?

Accountants can identify areas of wasteful spending and put together strategies to reduce unnecessary expenses. Look for answers that display logical and analytical thinking, with critical problem-solving skills. What to look for in an answer:

- Going the extra mile for their organisation
- Developing optimisation processes
- Reviewing historical data

Example: "I looked through the company's financial trends to discover redundancies in the business service contracts during slow seasons. By moving to a lower service tier when the extra capacity isn't needed, the company reduced costs by 15%."

This space is for notes

"Whenever you are blessed with a good thing, don't take it for granted. Whether it is a job, a relationship, money or whatever it is, be a good steward of it. Mismanage it or take it for granted and you will surely lose it."
Sterling Libs

HOW TO GET AND KEEP AN ACCOUNTING JOB

Identifying the skills that lead to success in accounting will not only increase your job satisfaction but also make it easier for you to build your long-term career goals.

No matter how big a company ever gets, the need for an accounts department persists. Perhaps that focus is on auditing, maybe management or tax and finance related. Chances are, you will start in one of two career paths – technical or commercial.

Accounting requires certain hard skills, such as mathematics and expertise with accounting software. Thorough knowledge of relevant laws and regulations is necessary for many positions, too.

However, accounting also requires some soft skills that you might not learn in school but will help you land and keep a job.

Here is a list of six accounting skills that employers are looking for in CV's/resumes, cover letters, job applications and interviews. It will serve you well to be in possession of these skills in increasing measure as you progress in your accounting career.

Staying current with technology is perhaps the most significant pressure you will continuously face in your accounting and finance career. As technology impacts on the way you do your job as an accountant, make sure you stay abreast of the changes and train and retrain to keep your skills up to date

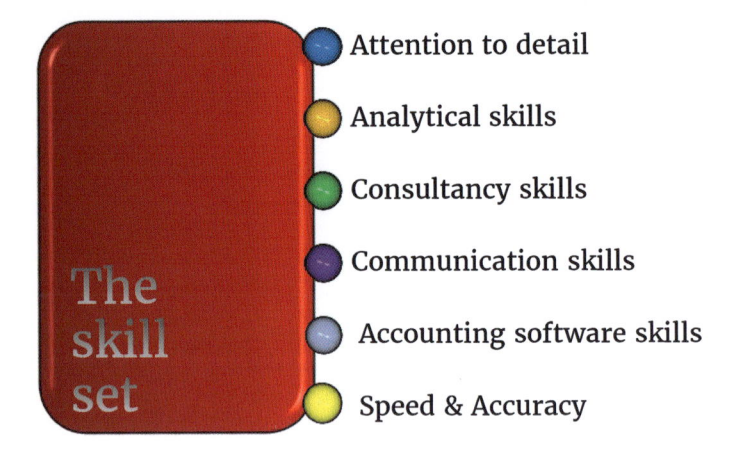

The skill set
- Attention to detail
- Analytical skills
- Consultancy skills
- Communication skills
- Accounting software skills
- Speed & Accuracy

And here is the professional code of ethics you are required to abide by as an accountant.

- Objectivity
- Confidentiality
- Integrity
- Professional competence & due care
- Adopting professional behaviour

Under the Code of Professional Ethics, as an accountant, you must follow these five principles:

1. **Integrity.**

You must be straightforward and honest in all professional and business relationships.

2. **Objectivity.**

You must not compromise professional or business judgment because of bias, conflict of interest or the undue influence of others.

3. **Professional competence and due care.**

You must maintain professional knowledge and skill (in practice, legislation and techniques) to ensure that a client or employer receives competent professional service.

4. **Confidentiality.**

You must not disclose confidential professional or business information or use it to your advantage unless you have explicit permission to disclose it, or a legal or professional right or duty to disclose it.

5. **Professional behaviour.**

You must comply with relevant laws and regulations and avoid any action that may bring disrepute to the profession.

Professional Ethics | AAT. (n.d.). Retrieved from https://www.aat.org.uk/about-aat/professional-ethics

The Top five things you should put on your CV

- *The CV needs to be relevant to your Job/company*
- *Show you have a range of experience*
- *Clearly state your qualifications*
- *Show you can respond to challenges*
- *Detail your achievements*

Qualifications like ACCA, CIMA, AAT, ICAEW will arm you with the knowledge and skills that project solid technical and professional capabilities.

When applying for roles, you need to find out where your strengths lie and what really interests you when applying for roles.

Take some time to do some work experience within a finance department and gain solid, relevant practical work experience in accountancy.

The Top five things to do during an interview

If you are successful in a job application and you are called for an interview, here are top five things you should do during your interview:

i. *Be honest – don't try to make up an answer if you don't know something.*
ii. *Show evidence of your competencies.*
iii. *Communicate clearly – eye contact, answering questions fully, using appropriate language are all important.*
iv. *Show passion for the company.*
v. *Be professional.*

Besides knowing what you should do at interviews, you should also know what you should not do at interviews. Here they are:

> Don't rush into giving an answer or response to a question, ensure you understand what's being asked and consider the context of the question.
> Do not go unprepared and make sure you have thought about the sort of questions you might be asked and have examples for each question.
> Refrain from using technical jargon where possible and talk about your contribution to a task, not just what your opinion or point of view on the subject.

This space is for notes

"Where are you going? And where are you coming from?"
Judges 19:17

WHY SOME PEOPLE STRUGGLE TO GET ACCOUNTING JOBS & WHAT TO DO ABOUT IT

Here are the top 7 reasons why some people are stuck and unable to get accounting jobs:

1. Lack of confidence in their accounting skills and fear of being rejected by employers.
2. Procrastination (putting things off till later).
3. Lack of focus – doing too many things at the same time but seeing little progress or results.
4. Lack of relevant UK practical work experience in accountancy.
5. Poor presentation. This is about your CV and interview skills. Would you say you have a great CV and excellent interview skills?
6. The sixth reason is that; people simply give up easily and quickly. There is a lack of persistence and patience, and the result is much frustration.
7. The seventh reason people struggle to get accounting jobs is inefficiency – unproductive use of their time, money and energy doing things that are not relevant or necessary to help them get an accounting job.

Are you facing any of the above seven challenges right now? If so, you don't have to continue struggling and feeling stuck. There is help available. TD&A Certified Accountants has been giving hands-on work experience for many, many accounting professionals for many years now and I am sure you could benefit from their practical work experience program. Click here to get in touch with them or visit www.tdanda.co.uk/careers

You can also book an appointment by Clicking here.

7 things you can do to help you get an accounting job quickly

If you are finding it hard to get an accounting job, there are a few things you can start doing today to help you move things a bit faster. We have helped hundreds of people breakthrough in their accounting career and get high earning accounting jobs. Here are some things you can start doing today to help you with your breakthrough.

1. Build your confidence – start by establishing exactly what kind of accounting job you want. Be clear and specific.
2. Secondly, prepare yourself, make plans for how you are going to solve or eliminate all the obstacles and limitations you are facing right now.
3. Remember to stay focused. I suggest you get a mentor and be disciplined. Do what you say you will do, on time and with enthusiasm.
4. You should also improve your professional skills – invest in yourself, get the relevant practical work experience in accountancy.
5. Market yourself effectively – post your CV to the right job boards and apply for jobs in the right companies. You need to be strategic about this, don't just randomly send your CV out there, you should make sure your CV reaches the right people when you send it and make sure you do follow-ups.
6. It is important to keep reviewing and reflecting on your progress. Know what is working and keep doing those things and stop doing the things that are not getting you the results you want.
7. Above all, persist, don't give up too soon. Your next application or interview may well be the one that changes everything. Don't lose hope.

There you have it. Do the above things, and you will be well on your way to making a huge difference in your accounting career job prospects.

If you need help and don't know where to start from, TD&A Certified Accountants can help you. Just get in touch with them by – clicking here.
Here is why I recommend TD&A Certified Accountants

ACCOUNTING JOB QUESTIONS AND ANSWERS

1. *They will train you in their accounting firm & help you get the practical work experience in accountancy,*
2. *They will be able to give you a professional reference from their accounting firm and also*
3. *Help you build your confidence and connect you to the right employers and recruitment agencies.*

Structure of their work experience

- The work experience is 100% practical
- It is done on a one to one basis online or in their office
- You will have a choice of accounting software such as Sage 50, Xero, QuickBooks and Excel to work with
- The duration of the work experience is between 1 month – one year and there is a fee applicable for doing any work experience program at TD&A.

Key requirements for you are:

- You need to be 18 years of age and above and
- You should also have studied or been studying accounting or bookkeeping course.

The accounting tasks you will get experience to do.

Their team of experienced accountants will train you one to one in the following accounting tasks:

1. Free software training - Choice of Xero, QuickBooks, Sage one and Sage 50 Accounts
2. Setting up account opening balances
3. Processing supplier invoices
4. processing customer invoices
5. Processing credit notes, write-offs and refunds
6. Recording customer receipts
7. processing supplier payments
8. Assisting with credit control
9. Managing petty cash
10. Payroll processing
11. Processing payroll journals
12. Preparing VAT returns
13. Doing bank reconciliations
14. Correcting errors in the general ledger

15. Working with spreadsheet/Excel – fundamentals
16. CV preparation and guidance on securing an accounting job
17. Doing balance sheet reconciliations
18. Doing Cash flow forecasting
19. Preparing yearend statutory accounts
20. Filing of the corporation tax return
21. Learn Pivot Tables & VLOOKUP
22. Preparing a set of management accounts

Further help and support

They will also help you to make a CV and offer you advice and tips on how to get an accounting job within a short period.

Even more, they also will give a professional reference from their firm to an employer or recruitment agency that will request it when employing you.

The work experience at TD&A will be perfect for you if the following apply to you:
- If lack of UK practical work experience in accountancy is stopping you from getting your ideal accounting job and if you are struggling and are just unsure what to do next, this work experience will be perfect for you.
- If you are getting lots of rejection from recruitment agencies and employers due to lack of practical work experience, then you have come to the right place, we can help you sort that out as soon as possible.
- If you are tired of working in a non-accounting related role and want to kickstart your accounting career, then this will help you get started.
- If you want to learn how to do month end account procedures, preparing year end accounts adequately, file a corporation tax return and annual reports to Companies House, prepare management accounts and do tax planning. Then this is definitely for you.
- You will also get the experience to help sign off your PER as well.

That's it, that's where I draw a line for now. I hope you followed through well. Mmmm...., Accounting - interesting, isn't it?

Thanks for giving me your time and attention, I hope it has been worth it for you.

AFTERWORD

It was a real honour speaking to you through the pages of this book. Thanks for listening to me.

If you found this book helpful, why not leave me your comment or feedback at sterling@sterlinglibs.com. I would really appreciate that.

I wish you a very fruitful and enjoyable career as an accountant and if our path happens to cross somewhere on this planet, come over and say hi.

If you want to understand more advanced stuff like how to do month end and how to prepare yearend accounts and tax returns check them out at www.sterlinglibs.com

Sterling.

ABOUT THE AUTHOR

Sterling Libs FCCA, is a fellow of the Association of Chartered Certified Accountants, a business consultant and a mentor.

He runs his accounting firm based in Canary Wharf London.

Sterling is so passionate about helping young aspiring accounting professionals to understand better how accounting is done in practice.

Through his accounting practice, he has championed UK practical work experience in accountancy training which has helped many individuals - (ACCA students & Affiliates, AAT students, CIMA students/Affiliates, university students and graduates in accounting) to get the work experience and accounting jobs in the UK.

Sterling is really gifted in making the seemingly complex simple, and throughout his books, he shows you fundamental and detailed illustrations with examples of how he does that.

He is an inspiring individual.

sterling@tdanda.co.uk

STERLING
LIBS

Printed in Great Britain
by Amazon

48064723R00041